The Ramblings of
A FATHER

The Ramblings of
A FATHER

DANIEL HARMESON

ARPress
45 Dan Road Suite 5
Canton MA 02021

Hotline: 1(888) 821-0229
Fax: 1(508) 545-7580

Ordering Information:
Quantity sales. Special discounts are available on quantity purchases by corporations, associations, and others. For details, contact the publisher at the address above.

Printed in the United States of America.

ISBN-13:   Paperback   979-8-89389-626-8
           eBook   979-8-89389-627-5

Library of Congress Control Number: 2024921456

Contents

To Touch You

Your smile is the sun.
Your laugh is the wind.
Your voice is the songs of the birds.
Your strength is the very ground I stand on.
Your beauty is reflected in the flowers around me.
To touch you, I need only to stand outside.

Write Me a Poem

Look into your mind and open the gate.
Don't ponder the words.
Why do you wait?
Pencil to hand; just begin to write.
Words flow to the paper, sometimes through the night.
Compose me a poem.
One that makes me cry.
You won't know you can do it,
Unless you try.

Remember When

Remember when we use to play?
Oh, how I wish those times could stay.
Life was so simple, pure, and fun.
We laughed, cried, and walked under the sun.
When bath time meant it was time for sleep.
Whispers in the dark; secrets to keep.
Best friends would greet us at the start of the morn.
A full day of exploring; new adventures born.
Where are those times, we cherished so dear?
A long time behind us, forgotten, I fear.
Glimpses of days past enter my dreams.
My friends long grown old; I can still hear their screams.
Oh, how I wish for those times again.
It's getting harder and harder; to remember when.

Country

Catfish, crawfish, and big ole bull frogs.
Shining at night, let's release the dogs.
Hot beer, cold beer, doesn't matter to us.
Sittin' on a tailgate just makin' a fuss.
Tank tops, blue jeans, bare foot y'all.
Shotguns, chainsaws, and burn pits in the fall.
Life in the country way out in the sticks,
Doesn't make us rednecks or even dumb hicks.
Yes Ma'am, yes Sir, thank yous' and please.
We just be good ole folks, who still pray from our knees.

Pondering

I sit here pondering out on my porch.
Toss'n back a cold one in the light of a Tiki torch.
Why is there air?
And how is it I can walk?
If we evolved from apes, why can't my dog Bo talk?
What makes a plane fly and not fall down?
Who thought to name a city, a building, and a town?
Where do the bubbles in a bottle of beer go?
Water from the sky; that turns to snow!?
When I say something wrong, my wife gets so mad.
The more I talk and explain things, the more I been had.
What, where, why, and continuous wondering.
All I can do is sit here, a-drinking and a- pondering.

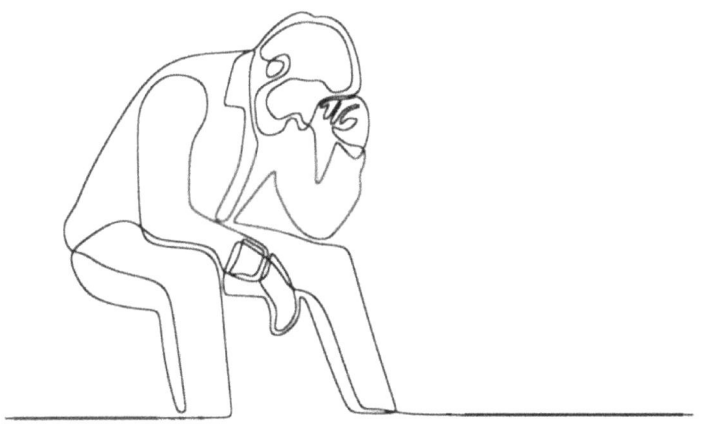

The Art of Conversation

My good friend and I sat in a bar.
Drinking and talking, we were the star.
Together we pooled both our IQ's.
Multiplied and doubled our brainpower by two's.
We were a sight, one for the ages.
As the beer flowed in, we grew smarter in stages.
Opinions, advice, the tongues were so quick.
Not sure if anything we said would sink in and stick.
But we talked and chatted to all who would listen.
A new world order, all leaders christened.
And by night's end this new revelation
Had bolstered our status and improved,
Our Art of Conversation.

The Little Man on My Shoulder

If I make it to be much older,
I owe it all to the little man on my shoulder.
For he is the one who stands watch over me
It is his voice I hear and stops what might be.
My moments of weakness and self-destruction
Hinder my path to positive production.
And when I enjoy the mind-altering juices,
I fall prey to so many terrible abuses.
I must train myself to be much bolder
And listen to The Little Man on My Shoulder.

Hurricane

The dark clouds loom overhead
and the wind begins to blow.
Heavy rain beats against the glass and the surf is high you know.
Hour after hour this disaster takes a toll and leaves its ugly mark.
Hunkered down inside a building no power has left you in the dark.
The mind begins to wonder will there be another day.
Anxiety turns to doubt, what games fear can play.
To hope for some comfort and much needed rest.
But you can't stop thinking of when the rivers will crest.
Must stay alert and fight the urge in case the worse comes true.
Think of all the good in life and picture the sky so blue.
All of a sudden it is quiet now, and an eerie calm arrives.
It's hard to imagine all the destruction that affects our very lives.
What is it that drives you to rebuild and makes you want to stay?
Knowing quite well another storm will plaque you again someday.

The Road of Life

I wander this road of life,
In search of its meaning.
Only to find a maze,
Of tributaries, constantly streaming.
The choices I make,
While many twist and turn.
Mistakes, failures, disappointments.
Only fuel my need to learn.
If only there was a map, and a book to guide.
This road of life
Would be an easy ride.

My Very Best Friend

My friend, my good friend, my very best friend.
I wasn't there for you at your end.
So, now I must write what you meant to me.
Your smile and words always set souls free.
Not a bad thought for all those around.
Through negative times, all positives found.
I miss your laugh and your infectious cheer.
I salute you and remember you,
I know you are near.

My God

Is my God all around me?
I cannot hear his voice.
How and why, I believe, is my unwavering choice.
I traveled to the mountains, way, way far,
Drove through the valleys alone in my car,
Sailed across the oceans, so green and so blue,
But I could not find my God.
Where are you?
It wasn't until I looked so deep into my heart,
'Tis then I found My God.
We were never really apart.

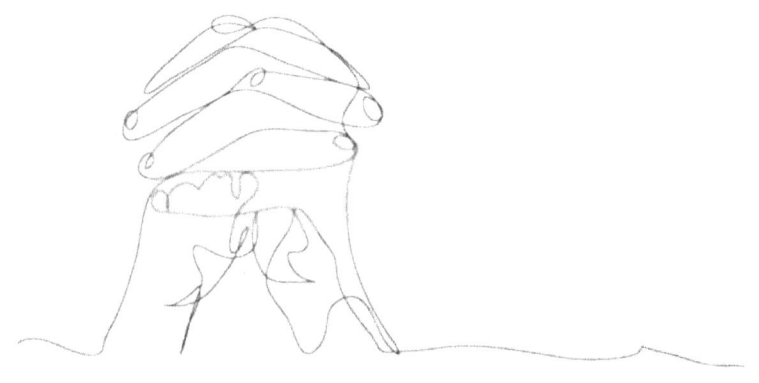

Living is Tough

It is not death that I fear
Or walking into that light.
But, living and doing
Always expected to be right.
Being the one to carry the load,
How can I continue to be so strong?
My might is weakening,
I fear I'll do wrong.
Decisions to make, all with great risk.
The roads I walk are long and rough.
People to please day after day.
Dying is easy.
It's living that's tough.

It's Okay

When all seems lost
And you're in trouble.
The bleakest of times
Multiply by double.
No worries, no frets,
Stay positive and true.
Stir all those good vibes,
And don't be blue.
For good times are near
And it's a new day.
The light is upon you,
It will be…OKAY!

On Again, Off Again

It was a time, oh so very long ago.
Together we were, day after day.
Cruising around on those old gravel roads,
How this would end we could not know.
But fate has a way of dividing a pair.
One walks north, so mature and true,
The other south, lost in youthful defiance.
No one ever said this life would be fair.
Those roads divided somehow reconverged.
On again and stronger from being apart.
Movies, parking, and hamburger joints,
Together we were more deeply submerged.
Now destiny has entered this fairy tale life,
Confusion, turbulence, and constant disappointments,
Stages of wrongdoings and mind-altered decisions,
Off again ends this troubled strife.
Life has a way of sorting things out.
As the years move by, the world goes on.
On again, off again, was actually no more,
Than what lessons in life are really all about.

I Stand

One moment I'm a boy,
Running barefoot on the road.
Not a care to bother me,
I bear no heavy load.
I play by day with all my friends.
And dream throughout the night.
Experiences have forged me,
Some wrong doings to make right.
The years go by, it seems so fast.
And I've grown so very tall.
No longer just a carefree child,
Now expected to know it all.
Circumstances can direct you,
And force you to play your hand.
I wait at the doorway of manhood,
Ready and willing to enter I stand.

Forgiveness

How can I reconcile
All that I did wrong?
To ask for forgiveness
May take too long.
Give me some time
To make it all right.
I won't give up
Not without a good fight.
Please listen to me
And look into your heart.
Don't have to forget,
But forgive, will be a good start.

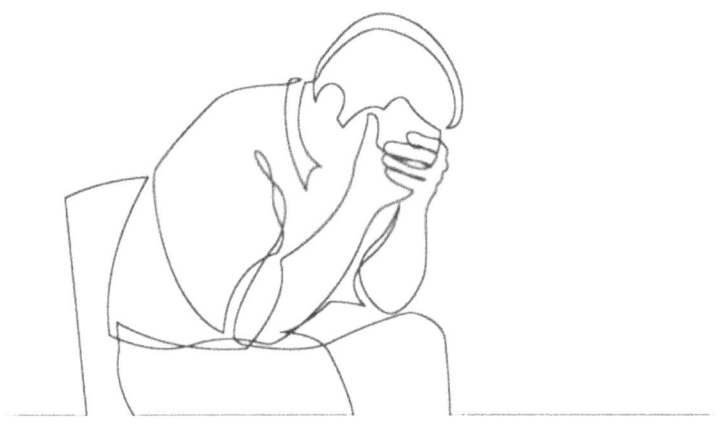

Demons

The Demons are here.
So very real.
They live in my mind.
Close enough to feel.
Push away, push away.
Got to block.
Can't shake their presence.
Heavy like a rock.
Be gone and leave me.
Peace is at hand.
For the moment they've left.
Lost in another land.

Our Way of Life

What is it about our world that others cannot understand?
Founded by rebels seeking freedom, they built a brand-new land.
Sacrifice, hard work, and tough decisions made.
The groundwork for Democracy was systematically laid.
The Words on those documents are what keeps this Country great.
Many times, our values have been tested, no greater as of late.
Somehow, someway, this Nation will endure and make it through this strife.
Good people, hard work, and smart decisions will preserve our way of life.

Brothers in Arms

To all of my brothers in arms,
Those from the cities, towns, and farms.
I am with you in spirit, along your side.
For I know what it's like to leave a family and a bride.
The dangers you face throughout the days,
Most cannot imagine what games fear plays.
Stay focused my brothers and bond with your friend.
Each other is all you have till the bitter end.
Come home to us all, we await your leave.
Some wait filled with happiness, while others grieve.
It takes more than mere words to prove you're brave.
So, be proud and stand tall.
For it is freedom we all crave.

Photograph of the author in Bosnia circa 1991

Brain Teaser

Where were you when I needed you today?
Gone somewhere, having a play?
Things to ponder, decisions to make.
Can't make this alone too much at stake.
Come back, come back; help me decide.
Not fair of you going along for the ride.
Need you to engage.
So, help me in kind.
That part of me.
Called my Mind!

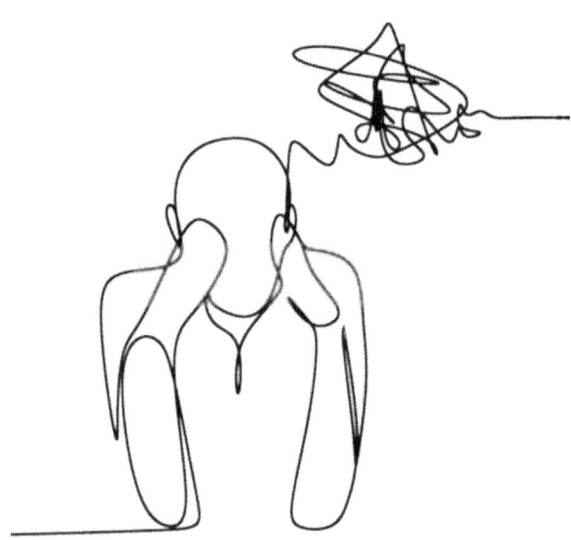

As I Should

My troubles are many
The thought process ain't right.
Got to make some adjustments,
Lots of Demons to fight.
Apologies to make,
The line is so long.
To fix all those things,
That I made wrong.
Cannot continue to operate this way,
Time is good. It's on my side.
Get it together before it's too late.
Life is too short, nowhere to hide.
For I promise to be better
And swear to be good.
Repent all my evil ways.
And live this life, as I should.

A single cloud passed by today
What secrets it must know
If only it would have stopped

A bush upon the desert floor
The sand of a shifting dune
I too am a lonely victim of time

The Pond

It is that time of the day when the sun is just right.
Your surface is so smooth, it's almost like glass.
The reflections of the trees, the clouds, and the birds,
Are majestic events, ones I do not want to pass.
Mesmerized by your beauty, your innocence, and life,
I can sit here for hours and gaze away the time.
Forget all the bad things and think of all the good.
I know you're just a pond, but a lovely one that's mine.

What Do You See?

Do you like what you see?
So, look long and hard.
Study that face.
What's behind those eyes?
Are you okay?
Do you want to flee?
What bothers you the most?
Can you sift through the haze?
Does it all make sense?
Or are you looking at a ghost?
What is it that you really fear?
Do truths outnumber all the lies?
Will you like what you discover?
Can you live with that person?
That stares back from the mirror?

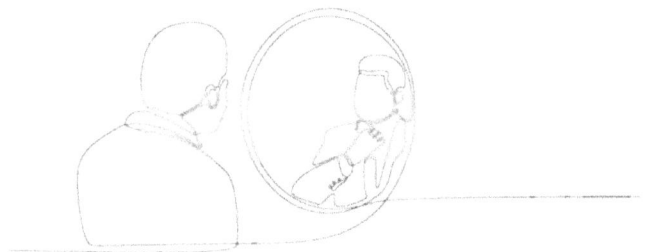

Weary

I am weary from burden
The load is too great.
Can't shoulder no more
What is my fate?
My mistakes and weaknesses
Far outnumber my strengths.
To hide all my faults
I go to great lengths.
Can someone please come,
And swoop me away.
I know I'll be better
Just get through the day.

The Words

Where are the words that need to be said?
Lost somewhere deep inside my head.
Feelings and emotions, both running so deep,
Must get them to come out, the climb is too steep.
Why won't they come and flow through my mouth?
Got to bring this to fruition, before it all goes south.
Practice and practice until they're so clear.
I must tell you now.
The words you long to hear.

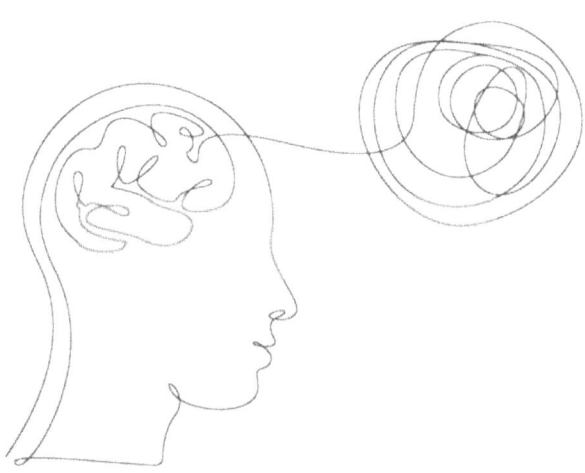

The Picture

The look from the picture that stares back at me
Renews my spirit and sets me free.
The innocence and love displayed in your eyes
Pushes me to be better, and more wise.
When I think all is wrong, and I am in doubt
That stare, that look,
Shows me what life is really all about.

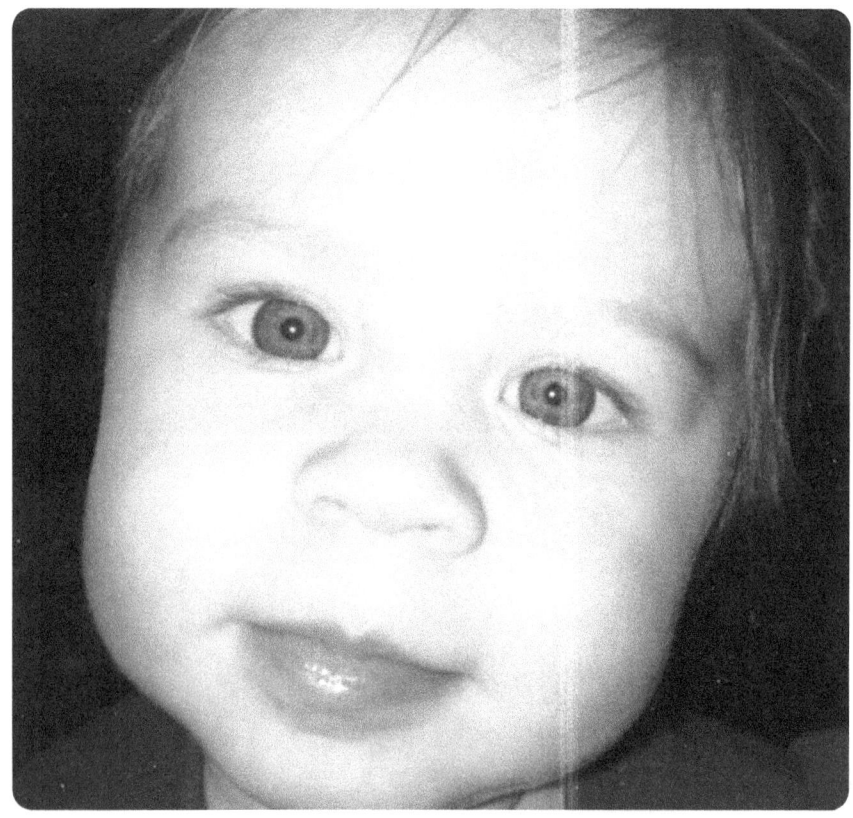

Dear Jasmine

The world can be so full of pain and gloom
But the Heavens saw fit to send you here.
Your smile and presence have lifted our souls
Gave hope to us all and made the flowers bloom.
Each time I see you and hold you so near
My heart just melts and my spirits lift.
Yes, angels exist and watch over us
So, time stands still, there is no fear.

Heaven Sent

God sent you from heaven late one night
Scared I would and could not do right.
So tiny, so frail, that you were
To hold you and touch you, not sure.
But you grew and became so very strong.
I knew then you could do no wrong.
To be your father and give you Love
Is something special, from way above.

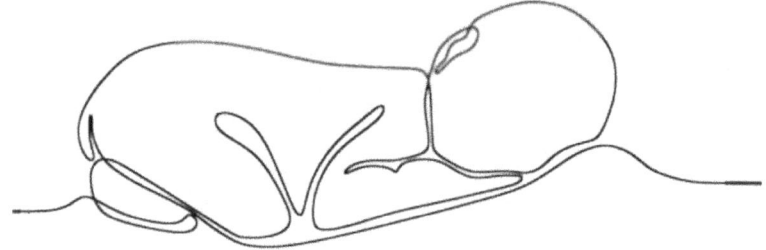

Shining Star

You were the one
I thought would be a son.
But the angels said, "oh, nay"
A girl is due today.
No matter, I was just as proud
You arrived and were very loud.
Strong and determined, that you were
Something special to be, I was sure.
To watch you grow into what you are
You have become my shining star.

When I'm Gone

When the time comes for me to leave
Don't cry for me woman, or even grieve.
Rejoice in knowing together we were.
Our love was real that's for sure.
You were right more than you were wrong.
I should have told you in a poem or a song.
The sacrifices you made, the life you surrendered,
Will stay with me now, always remembered.
What can I do to make it all good?
Now that I'm gone, I wish I could.

In the End

Memories of times long gone by.
Have sharpened my perspective of who am I.
Hard lessons learned both good and bad.
Some filled with joy, others very sad.
What is it that shapes my feeble mind?
Makes me want to be loving, caring, and kind.
Through the people I meet experiences abound.
Defines the soul, until it is I who am found.
This circle of life that does not bend,
I can only hope to be remembered in the end.

The clouds move by, day turns to night
The world evolves
Will humanity survive

A New Day Begins

Close your eyes and listen to the silence.
The world stops moving, as if in defiance.
That moment of peace that fills your soul,
Recoups, refreshes, and makes you whole.
As if by magic sent down from space,
All the ugly is gone, new hope in its place.
So, wake up now, and open your eyes.
A new day begins, cleansed by the skies.

www.ingramcontent.com/pod-product-compliance
Lightning Source LLC
Chambersburg PA
CBHW061721120626
46550CB00003B/1319